THIS WILD
AND PRECIOUS LIFE

A Journal

MARY OLIVER

THIS WILD
AND PRECIOUS LIFE

A Journal

MARY OLIVER

CLARKSON POTTER/PUBLISHERS

New York

THIS WILD AND PRECIOUS
LIFE BELONGS TO

Who made the world?

Who made the swan and the black bear?

Who made the grasshopper?

This grasshopper, I mean—

the one who has flung herself out of the grass,

the one who is eating sugar out of my hand,

who is moving her jaws back and forth instead of up and down—

who is gazing around with her enormous and complicated eyes.

Now she lifts her pale forearms and thoroughly washes her face.

Now she snaps her wings open, and floats away.

I don't know exactly what a prayer is.

I do know how to pay attention, how to fall down

into the grass, how to kneel down in the grass,

how to be idle and blessed, how to stroll through the fields,

which is what I have been doing all day.

Tell me, what else should I have done?

Doesn't everything die at last, and too soon?

Tell me, what is it you plan to do

with your one wild and precious life?

Bless the notebook that I always carry in
    my pocket.
And the pen.
Bless the words with which I try to say
    what I see, think, or feel.
With gratitude for the grace of the earth.
The expected and the exception, both.
For all the hours I have been given to
    be in this world.

—FROM "GOOD MORNING"

Six black ibis
step through the black and mossy panels
of summer water.

Six times
I sigh with delight.

Keep looking.

—FROM "SAND DABS, THREE"

Let the path become where I choose to walk,
and not otherwise established.

—FROM "ON NOT MOWING THE LAWN"

If you suddenly and unexpectedly feel joy,
don't hesitate. Give in to it.

. . .

Joy is not made to be a crumb.

—FROM "DON'T HESITATE"

Is it true that the wind
streaming especially in fall
through the pines
is saying nothing, nothing at all,

or is it just that I don't yet know the language?

—"WIND IN THE PINES"

Instructions for living a life:

Pay attention.

Be astonished.

Tell about it.

—FROM "SOMETIMES"

What can we do,

but keep on breathing in and out,

modest and willing, and in our places?

—FROM "STARS"

light of the world, hold me.

—FROM "THAT SWEET FLUTE JOHN CLARE"

Today is a day of
dark clouds and slow rain.
The little blades of corn
are so happy.

—"TODAY"

As long as you're dancing, you can
      break the rules.
Sometimes breaking the rules is just
      extending the rules.

Sometimes there are no rules.

—"THREE THINGS TO REMEMBER"

Hello, sun in my face.
Hello, you who make the morning
and spread it over the fields
and into the faces of the tulips
and the nodding morning glories,
and into the windows of, even, the
miserable and the crotchety—

best preacher that ever was,
dear star, that just happens
to be where you are in the universe
to keep us from ever-darkness,
to ease us with warm touching,
to hold us in the great hands of light—
good morning, good morning, good morning.

Watch, now, how I start the day
in happiness, in kindness.

Don't bother me.

I've just

been born.

You must not ever stop being whimsical.

. . .

And you must not, ever, give anyone else
the responsibility for your life.

—FROM "STAYING ALIVE"

The sea can do craziness, it can do smooth,
it can lie down like silk breathing
or toss havoc shoreward; it can give

gifts or withhold all; it can rise, ebb, froth
like an incoming frenzy of fountains, or it can
sweet-talk entirely. As I can too,

and so, no doubt, can you, and you.

it is a serious thing

just to be alive
    on this fresh morning
        in this broken world.

—FROM "INVITATION"

Sometimes I really believe it, that I am going to
save my life

a little.

—FROM "THE RETURN"

Love yourself. Then forget it. Then, love the world.

—FROM "TO BEGIN WITH, THE SWEET GRASS"

You don't ever know where
a sentence will take you, depending
on its roll and fold.

—FROM "FOX"

What did you notice?
The dew-snail;

the low-flying sparrow;

the bat, on the wind, in the dark;

big-chested geese, in the V of sleekest performance;

the soft toad, patient in the hot sand;

the sweet-hungry ants;

the uproar of mice in the empty house;

the tin music of the cricket's body;

the blouse of the goldenrod.

What did you hear?
The thrush greeting the morning;

the little bluebirds in their hot box;

the salty talk of the wren,

then the deep cup of the hour of silence.

What did you admire?
The oaks, letting down their dark and hairy fruit;

the carrot, rising in its elongated waist;

the onion, sheet after sheet, curved inward to the
     pale green wand;

at the end of summer the brassy dust, the almost liquid
     beauty of the flowers;

then the ferns, scrawned black by the frost.

What astonished you?
The swallows making their dip and turn over the water.

—FROM "GRATITUDE"

Is the soul solid, like iron?
Or is it tender and breakable, like
the wings of a moth in the beak of the owl?

—FROM "SOME QUESTIONS YOU MIGHT ASK"

What is s so utterly invisible
as tomorrow?

—FROM "WALKING TO OAK HEAD POND, AND THINKING OF
THE PONDS I WILL VISIT IN THE NEXT DAYS AND WEEKS"

The multiplicity of forms! The hummingbird,
the fox, the raven, the sparrow hawk, the
otter, the dragonfly, the water lily! And
on and on. It must be a great disappointment
to God if we are not dazzled at least ten
times a day.

—FROM "GOOD MORNING"

Meadowlark, when you sing it's as if

you lay your yellow breast upon mine and say

hello, hello, and are we not

of one family, in our delight of life?

—FROM "MEADOWLARK SINGS AND I GREET HIM IN RETURN"

Now that I am free to be myself, who am I?

—FROM "BLUE IRIS"

Listen, whatever you see and love—
that's where you are.

—FROM "LUKE'S JUNKYARD SONG"

Do you bow your head when you pray or do you look
 up into that blue space?
Take your choice, prayers fly from all directions.

—FROM "WHISTLING SWANS"

What would you like to see again?
My dog: her energy and exuberance, her willingness,
    her language beyond all nimbleness of tongue, her
    recklessness, her loyalty, her sweetness, her
    strong legs, her curled black lip, her snap.

What was most tender?
Queen Anne's lace, with its parsnip root;
the everlasting in its bonnets of wool;
the kinks and turns of the tupelo's body;
the tall, blank banks of sand;
the clam, clamped down.

What was most wonderful?
The sea, and its wild shoulders;
the sea and its triangles;
the sea lying back on its long athlete's spine.

What did you think was happening?
The green breast of the hummingbird;
the eye of the pond;
the wet face of the lily;
the bright, puckered knee of the broken oak;
the red tulip of the fox's mouth;
the up-swing, the down-pour, the frayed sleeve
of the first snow—

so the gods shake us from our sleep.

—FROM "GRATITUDE

Listen, whatever it is you try
to do with your life, nothing will ever dazzle you
like the dreams of your body

—FROM "HUMPBACKS"

There are things you can't reach. But
you can reach out to them, and all day long.

The wind, the bird flying away. The idea of God.

—FROM "WHERE DOES THE TEMPLE BEGIN, WHERE DOES IT END?"

You are young. So you know everything. You leap into the boat and begin rowing. But, listen to me. Without fanfare, without embarrassment, without any doubt, I talk directly to your soul. Listen to me. Lift the oars from the water, let your arms rest, and your heart, and heart's little intelligence, and listen to me. There is life without love. It is not worth a bent penny, or a scuffed shoe. It is not worth the body of a dead dog nine days unburied. When you hear, a mile away and still out of sight, the churn of the water as it begins to swirl and roil, fretting around the sharp rocks—when you hear that unmistakable pounding—when you feel the mist on your mouth and sense ahead the embattlement, the long falls plunging and streaming—then row, row for your life toward it.

—FROM "WEST WIND"

Who can tell how lovely in June is the
        honey locust tree, or why
a tree should be so sweet and live
        in this world?

—FROM "HONEY LOCUST"

If you think you see a face in the clouds, why not
send a greeting? It can't do any harm.

—FROM "A LITTLE ADO ABOUT THIS AND THAT"

We are all wild, valorous, amazing.

—FROM "A FEW WORDS"

Therefore tell me:

what will engage you?

What will open the dark fields of your mind,

 like a lover

  at first touching?

—FROM "FLARE"

Am I not among the early risers
and the long-distance walkers?

Have I not stood, amazed, as I consider
the perfection of the morning star
above the peaks of the houses, and the crowns of the trees
        blue in the first light?
Do I not see how the trees tremble, as though
        sheets of water flowed over them
though it is only wind, that common thing
        free to everyone, and everything?

—FROM "AM I NOT AMONG THE EARLY RISERS"

What would the world be like without music or
rivers or the green and tender grass? What would
this world be like without dogs?

—FROM "DOG TALK"

what does it mean, that the world is beautiful—

what does it mean?

—FROM "GRAVEL"

Look, hasn't my body already felt
like the body of a flower?

Look, I want to love this world
as though it's the last chance I'm ever going to get
to be alive
and know it.

—FROM "OCTOBER"

I don't know where prayers go,
or what they do.

Do cats pray, while they sleep
half-asleep in the sun?

—FROM "I HAPPENED TO BE STANDING"

Have I lived enough?
Have I loved enough?

—FROM "THE GARDENER"

Everybody needs a safe place.

—FROM "EVERY DOG'S STORY"

What happens
to the leaves after
they turn red and golden and fall
away? What happens

to the singing birds
when they can't sing
any longer? What happens
to their quick wings?

Do you think there is any
personal heaven
for any of us?
Do you think anyone,

the other side of that darkness,
will call to us, meaning us?

—FROM "ROSES, LATE SUMMER"

All my life I have been able to feel happiness,

except whatever was not happiness,

which I also remember.

Each of us wears a shadow.

—FROM "THE POND"

Does the hummingbird think he himself invented his crimson throat?
He is wiser than that, I think.

—FROM "HER GRAVE"

Every day
  I see or I hear
    something
      that more or less

kills me
  with delight,
    that leaves me
      like a needle

in the haystack
  of light.

—FROM "MINDFUL"

Do stones feel?

Do they love their life?

Or does their patience drown out everything else?

—FROM "DO STONES FEEL?"

What should we say

      is the truth of the world?

         The miles alone

in the pinched dark?

   or the push of the promise?

—FROM "THE BOBCAT"

Doesn't anybody in
the world anymore want to get up in the

middle of the night and
sing?

—FROM "UPSTREAM"

Where are you when you're not thinking?
Frightening, isn't it?
Where are you when you're not feeling anything?
Oh, worse!

—FROM "MORE EVIDENCE"

This morning, at waterside, a sparrow flew
to a water rock and landed, by error, on the back
of an eider duck; lightly it fluttered off, amused.
the duck, too, was not provoked, but, you might say, was
laughing.

This afternoon a gull sailing over
our house was casually scratching
its stomach of white feathers with one
pink foot as it flew.

Oh Lord, how shining and festive is your gift to us, if we
only look, and see.

Sometimes I need
    only to stand
        wherever I am
            to be blessed.

—FROM "IT WAS EARLY"

What is my name,
o what is my name
that I may offer it back
to the beautiful world?

—FROM "FROM THE BOOK OF TIME"

I go down to the shore in the morning
and depending on the hour the waves
are rolling in or moving out,
and I say, oh I am miserable,
what shall—
what should I do? And the sea says
in its lovely voice:
Excuse me, I have work to do.

Will somebody or something please start to sing?

—FROM "THE ROSES"

Can you imagine a world without certainty?
The wind rises and the wind falls.

—FROM "GRAVEL"

Are you afraid?
　　　Somewhere a thousand swans are flying
　　　　　through the winter's worst storm.

—FROM "GRAVEL"

Slowly
up the hill,
like a thicket of white flowers,
forever
is coming.

—FROM "GRAVEL"

WILD GEESE

You do not have to be good.
You do not have to walk on your knees
for a hundred miles through the desert, repenting.
You only have to let the soft animal of your body
        love what it loves.
Tell me about despair, yours, and I will tell you mine.
Meanwhile the world goes on.
Meanwhile the sun and the clear pebbles of the rain
are moving across the landscapes,
over the prairies and the deep trees,
the mountains and the rivers.
Meanwhile the wild geese, high in the clean blue air,
are heading home again.
Whoever you are, no matter how lonely,
the world offers itself to your imagination,
calls to you like the wild geese, harsh and exciting—
over and over announcing your place
in the family of things.

Was I lost? No question.

Did I know where I was? Not at all.

Had I ever been happier in my life? Never.

REFERENCES

Mary Oliver Poems and Poetry Collections

American Primitive (1983)

"Humpbacks"

"The Bobcat"

Dream Work (1986)

"One or Two Things"

"Wild Geese"

House of Light (1990)

"Roses, Late Summer"

"The Summer Day"

Blue Pastures (1995)

"A Few Words"

"Staying Alive"

West Wind (1997)

"Am I Not Among the Early Risers"

"Fox"

"Sand Dabs, Three"

"Stars"

"That Sweet Flute John Clare"

"West Wind"

The Leaf and the Cloud (2000)

"Flare"

"From the Book of Time"

"Gravel"

What Do We Know (2002)

"Blue Iris"

"Gratitude"

"The Return"

"Walking to Oak Head Pond, and Thinking of the Ponds I Will Visit in the Next Days and Weeks"

Why I Wake Early (2004)

"Look and See"

"Mindful"

"Where Does the Temple Begin, Where Does It End?"

"Why I Wake Early"

Blue Iris (2004)

"October"

"Some Questions You Might Ask"

"The Roses"

"Upstream"

New and Selected Poems:
Volume Two (2005)
  "Honey Locust"

Red Bird (2008)
  "Invitation"
  *"Meadowlark Sings and I Greet Him
  in Return"*
  "Sometimes"

Evidence (2009)
  "It Was Early"
  "To Begin With, the Sweet Grass"

Swan (2010)
  "Don't Hesitate"
  *"Mist in the Morning, Nothing
  Around Me but Sand and Roses"*
  "More Evidence"
  "Today"
  "Wind in the Pines"

A Thousand Mornings (2012)
  "I Go Down to the Shore"
  "I Happened to Be Standing"
  "The Gardener"
  *"The Poet Compares Human Nature to the
  Ocean From Which We Came"*
  "Three Things to Remember"

Dog Songs (2013)
  "Dog Talk"
  "Every Dog's Story"
  "Her Grave"
  "Luke's Junkyard Song"

Blue Horses (2014)
  "A Little Ado About This and That"
  "Do Stones Feel?"
  "Good Morning"
  "On Not Mowing the Lawn"

Felicity (2015)
  "The Pond"
  "Whistling Swans"

Copyright © 2024 by NW Orchard LLC
Illustrations © 2024 by Kathryn Hunter

Published in the United States by Clarkson Potter/Publishers,
an imprint of the Crown Publishing Group,
a division of Penguin Random House LLC, New York.
CLARKSONPOTTER.COM

CLARKSON POTTER is a trademark and POTTER with colophon
is a registered trademark of Penguin Random House LLC.

Selected material originally appeared in previous publications
listed on pages 206-207.

ISBN: 978-0-593-58028-8

Printed in China

Editors: Sara Neville and Lindley Boegehold
Designer: Lise Sukhu
Art director: Danielle Deschenes
Production manager: Jessica Heim
Compositors: Dix and Zoe Tokushige
Marketer: Chloe Aryeh

10 9 8 7 6 5 4 3 2

First Edition